The Siege of Ladysmith

2 November 1899 -
28 February 1900

Steve Watt

RAVAN PRESS

The Battle Book Series

- The Battle of Talana
- The Battle of Elandslaagte
- The Battle of Colenso
- The Battle of Spioenkop
- The Battle of Vaalkrans
- The Battle of the Thukela Heights
- The Siege of Ladysmith

First published in 1999

Ravan Press
P O Box 145, Randburg 2125

ISBN: 0 86975 519 6

DTP and design by: Heather Brooksbank, Resolution

Cover Design: David Selfe, Dark Horse Design

Cartography: Toni Bodington & Olive Anderson
Cartographic Unit, University of Natal (Pietermaritzburg)

Photographs and sketches from: the KwaZulu-Natal Provincial Museum Service Collection

Lithographic repro by: 3 White Dogs

Contents

Anglo-Boer War Sites

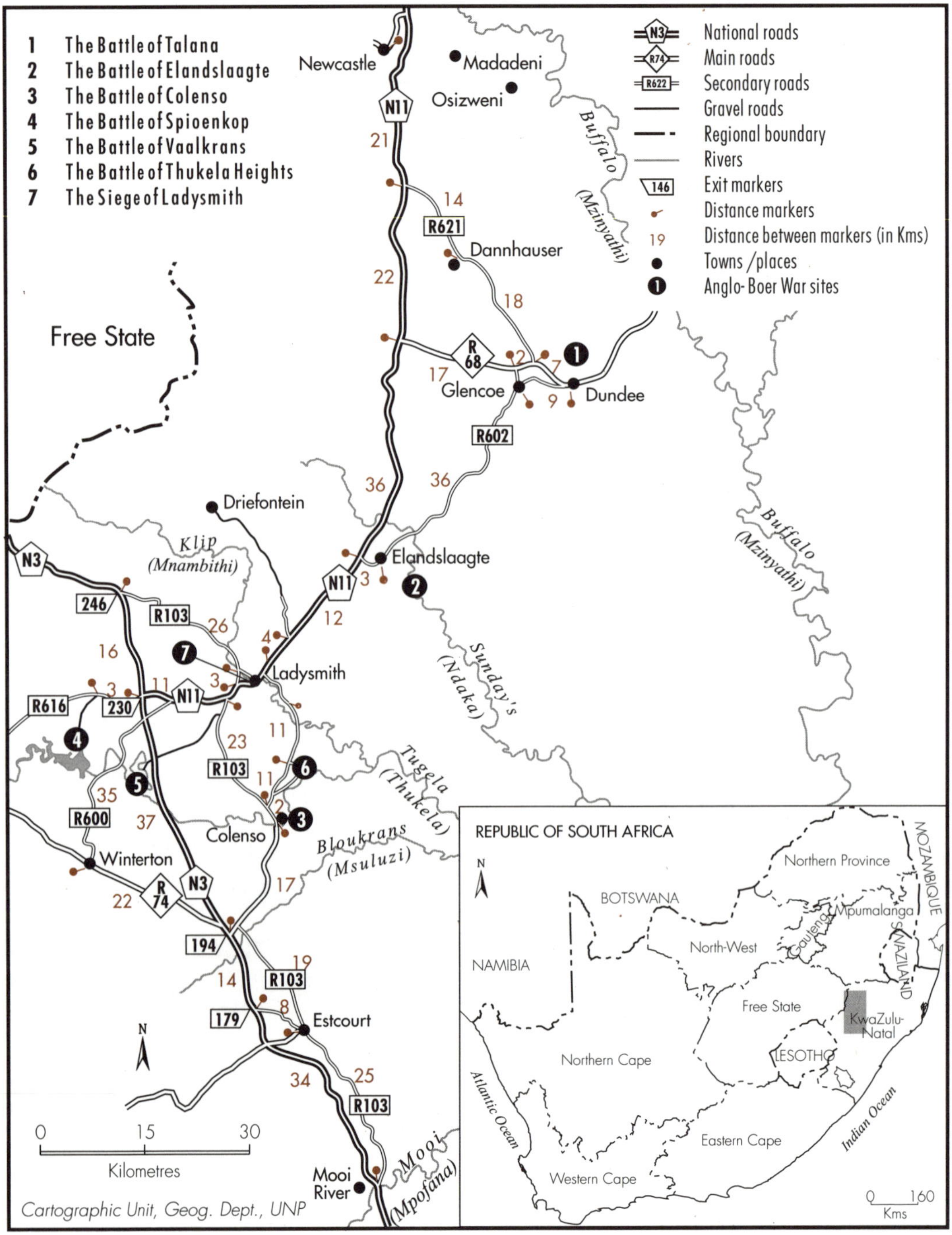

Preface

This Battle Book series has been written to make information, photographs and maps of the most significant Anglo-Boer War sites in KwaZulu-Natal more readily available.

The books are not exhaustive studies of the various sites but rather field guides, designed to assist the reader in interpreting the terrain and understanding the events.

Although the Battle Books form a series, each book has been fully contextualised and can be followed on its own.

Contributors to this series share a long-term interest in the Anglo-Boer War and have each made their own unique contribution to the historiography and understanding of the conflict. With the assistance of an editorial committee, every effort has been made to maintain balance and accuracy.

A slightly flexible approach has been adopted to the spelling of names. As a general rule, the most recent spelling utilised on the state's Survey and Mapping 1:50 000 maps has been adopted. Thus for instance Laing's Nek becomes Lang's Nek. Where the name used to describe a topographical feature differs significantly from that in the historical literature to that appearing on the map, then the one used in the books and documents is adopted. The spelling of the river Thukela (Tugela) presents a slight problem. On the maps it is spelt as given in the brackets. However, in most current academic historical literature the former form has been adopted, which spelling has been followed in this series of books.

Background

On 11 October 1899 the Anglo-Boer War began with the Boer invasion of the Natal and Cape colonies. Nowhere, from a Boer point of view, did the situation call more urgently for immediate action than on the Natal border. Both the Transvaal commandos and those from the Orange Free State invaded Natal via the passes in the Drakensberg.

It was obvious to the Natal government that the Boers were planning to cut off all the British forces north of the Thukela River. Major-General Sir William Penn Symons, with a force concentrated in Dundee, declined to retire to Ladysmith, where a larger force under Lieutenant-General Sir George White VC had gathered. Symons hoped that he could hold Dundee.

The Boers attacked Dundee from Talana Hill (20 October 1899), and although repulsed, Brigadier-General Yule, on whom devolved the comand (Symons being mortally wounded), decided to withdraw to Ladysmith. In an effort to restore railway communication with Dundee, White attacked the Boers at Elandslaagte (21 October 1899), where the Boers were driven off. After receipt of the news about the Boer reverse, the Free State commandos were ordered to Elandslaagte. The arrival of the enemy on the heights north of Ladysmith increased White's anxiety for the safety of the British column retiring from Dundee. There followed an engagement at Rietfontein (24 October 1899). This was an inconclusive event with neither side claiming victory. The British retired to Ladysmith and the Boers advanced unopposed on the town uniting their forces for a planned encirclement. White responded with an attack on the Boers to the north and east of the town, but was repulsed (30 October).

On 1 November at a council of war, attended by the Transvaal and Free State Commandants, it was resolved that their commandos

Dutch medical personnel assisting the Boers during the siege. They were stationed at Modderspruit, just north of Ladysmith.

should besiege Ladysmith and prevent the escape of White's force. They hoped to bring about the surrender of the garrison with an artillery bombardment, before many days passed.

Although a siege would paralyse his power of offence, White, with his force in Ladysmith, hoped to detain the bulk of the Boer invading forces north of the Thukela river, and thereby to save Pietermaritzburg and Durban from falling into the hands of the Boers. Whilst retreat across the Thukela was still possible, White considered that such a venture would be too risky. It was thought that the nature of the country favoured the Boers. The events on 30 October had shaken the British commander's belief in the striking power of his force. White was also impressed by the numbers of Boers present and their mobility.

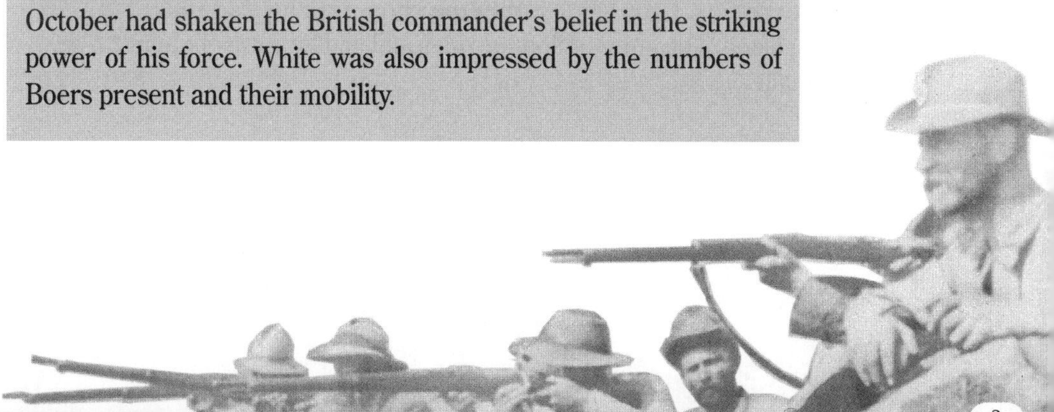

The Long Tom guns, French made Creusot 155mm guns, fired a shell weighing 46 kilograms with a range of just over 10 kilometres.

Ladysmith besieged

From Pepworth Hill the Boer artillery bombardment of the town started at 05:30 on 30 October 1899. The most noteworthy piece was the 155 mm Creusot, soon to be dubbed "Long Tom" which fired a 46 kg shell over a range of more than 10 kilometres. Three days later a British reconnaissance force advanced in a south-westerly direction and drew fire from a Boer force beyond Middle Hill. The British lost five men killed, including two officers, and 28 wounded. The Boer encirclement of Ladysmith was complete and had trapped 13 745 Imperial troops with 51 guns, 18 machine guns and about 7 600 civilians in it. The siege became effective from 2 November 1899.

White had more than sufficient stores to feed the troops and civilians for three months. Requisitions from the shops and hotels brought in additional food. The ammunition for rifles and artillery was thought to be adequate.

The Long Tom gun was used on Mbulwana Hill for most of the siege and from this emplacement proved a constant threat to the town's inhabitants.

Other than shelling the town into submission the Boers had no other ideas on how to bring about the fall of Ladysmith. The most practical way was to storm the town, but the defenders had now become firmly entrenched along a perimeter of 22 kilometres. In and around Ladysmith the hills provided a natural defensive position, the soldiers giving names to various prominences: Devonshire Post, Helpmekaar Hill, Cemetery Hill, Tunnel Hill, Junction Hill, Gordon Hill, Cove Redoubt, Leicester Post, King's Post, Ration Post, Rifleman's Post, Red Hill, Signpost Ridge, Maiden Castle, Caesar's Camp, Wagon Point, Wagon Hill (see map). The town consisted of two main streets, two hotels, shops and houses sporting corrugated iron roofs. During the early stages, the British artillery was emplaced along the northern defences. The most significant British guns were the 4.7-inch [120 mm] naval guns, one of which was positioned on a hill called Cove Redoubt and named the "Princess Victoria Battery", while the other was on Junction Hill and called "Lady Anne".

"Lady Anne", an answer to Long Tom? This 4.7 inch naval gun was called "Lady Anne". The ranges of these naval guns were the only ones which almost matched those of the Long Toms.

Ladysmith, with its natural defensive position, is surrounded by an undulating plain bounded by an almost concentric chain of hills, on which the Boers were stationed. The most noteworthy were Thornhill's Kop, Vaalkop (called Surprise Hill by the British), Tchrengula, Bell's Kop, Pepworth Hill, Long Hill, Lombard's Kop with its spur Gun Hill, Mbulwana, End Hill, Middle Hill, Mounted Infantry Hill, Lancers Hill, Rifleman's Ridge (called Blaauwbank by the Boers) and Telegraph Ridge.

After a Boer force headed southward into Natal, there remained 9 900 men in the environs of Ladysmith. They eventually had 22 guns, including the 155 mm Creusot (Long Tom).

The Boer bombardment of Ladysmith began in earnest on 2 November when the Long Tom opened fire on the town and then on to Junction Hill mortally wounding an officer, Lieutenant FG Egerton.

Imperial Light Horse camp on the banks of the Klip River in November 1899. Seeking shelter from the Boer shells.

Shelling the town into submission?

A demonstration by the Boers against Devonshire Post, followed by an intense bombardment, led to a meeting of the Town Council. They decided that the non-combatants and ill soldiers should be removed to a place of safety. A request to Commandant-General Piet Joubert, commander of the Zuid-Afrikaansche Republiek (Transvaal) commandos, that the civilians and the infirm be evacuated from the town was refused. Instead, permission was granted to establish a neutral camp 6 km from town, but still inside the siege lines. This proposal was accepted by the

Hospital tents at Intombi camp

British authorities, and during early November a large field hospital, initially with 300 beds and a camp for non-combatants was established, all under canvas, near Intombi Spruit. Several civilians refused this offer and remained in the town.

On 8 November another Long Tom opened fire from the top of Mbulwana. In general the Boer bombardment was confined to daylight hours, Monday to Saturday. For protection from Boer shells the garrison improved its defensive works seeking shelter behind stone sangars, while some civilians dug caverns into the banks of the Klip River. In spite of the measures taken to ensure maximum safety, the bombardment nevertheless proved trying to the nerves of the garrison and was not without mishap. For example, on 14 November a trooper of the Natal Mounted Rifles was killed in his tent, and five days later Dr Stark, a civilian, was killed in front of the Royal Hotel. On 24 November three men of the Liverpool Regiment were killed and eight wounded (three mortally). Six days later a shell struck the Town Hall, then used as a hospital, killing one patient and wounding nine others. Until 5 December no fewer than 4 200 Boer shells were fired into the town, killing 31 soldiers and wounding 145, while the civilians' death list was fewer than 40. Donald Macdonald, a journalist in the siege, relates:

> "Those who were a little bit afraid at first became quite indifferent; others, who were very much afraid began to regard themselves as, upon the whole, rather brave. The actual number of deaths was not great, but every man went out of a morning with a feeling that it might be his turn, and experience had convinced him, too, that ordinary precautions were useless, death came impartially. Sometimes a man rode gaily into his shell, at others he stood still and patiently waited for it... but everyone was more or less harassed, even if advantaged by narrow escapes."

W T Maud and the late C W Steevens journalists with the Graphic *and* Daily Mail *respectively, digging a bomb-proof shelter in the Ladysmith correspondents' camp, 5 November 1899.*

Shelling by the Boers was a constant threat. This is the interior of Sutton's Store after a shell burst in it.

For the town's inhabitants there were sufficient protective works against shellfire. Several camps had their own signalman whose duty was to watch for any indication of bombardment, and then sound the alarm. In particular the Long Tom on Mbulwana, called "Puffing Billy", was carefully watched. After firing, characterised by a puff of white smoke, there was an interval of 20-22 seconds before the arrival of the shell. Despite the precautions taken the garrison continued to suffer casualties. The most noteworthy of these were: on 18 November a single shell from Mbulwana killed four Natal Carbineers and wounded seven. Three days later a shell struck the headquarters of the British commander in Poort Road, after which he moved to safer quarters on Convent Hill. On 22 November another shell from

Mbulwana hit a position amongst the Gloucester Regiment, killing nine men and wounding three. For the period 12-31 December, 26 soldiers were killed or died of wounds and 52 were wounded. Several public buildings, including the Town Hall and Royal Hotel, were either destroyed or damaged. Against the Boer bombardment White was virtually defenceless in spite of the preponderance of artillery. The only artillery which could effectively reach the Boer artillery were two 4.7-inch naval guns.

Parbhoo Singh was an indentured labourer employed by the Dundee Coal Mine. It was his task during the siege to signal whenever he saw a flash from one of the Boer Long Toms. About 22 seconds elapsed before the shell burst over the town. Singh was given a Kashmir robe by the Viceroy of India in recognition of the brave task he carried out in the war. The robe was presented to him in the Durban City Hall during a special function on 11 October 1900.

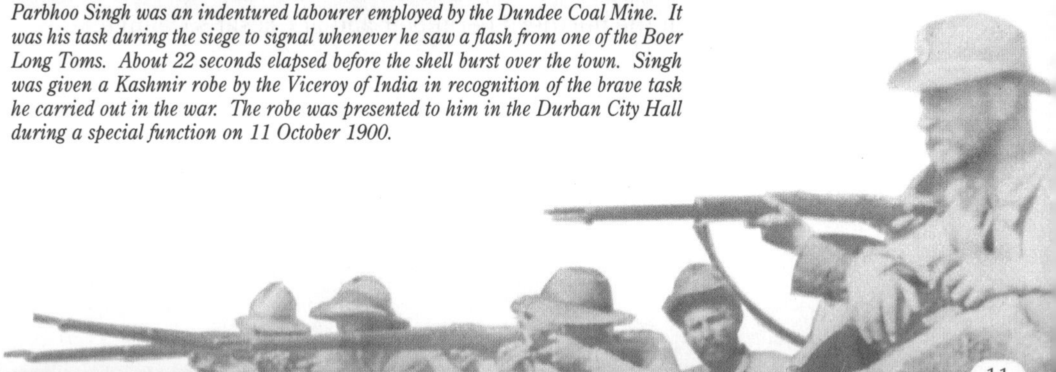

An Indian bakery during the siege.

Playing cat and mouse

After a week of bombardment, the garrison in the town showed no signs of surrendering. The tactic of shelling White's force into submission would have to be replaced by one of active offence. The Boers hoped that this would place them in possession of some point of the defence line from where they could bring about the fall of the town. On 9 November Ladysmith was bombarded in earnest, and heavy Boer rifle fire was directed at Observation Hill on the northern perimeter and at Caesar's Camp in

the south. The British replied with rifle and artillery fire from the threatened points. However, although the Boer shooting continued for the rest of the day, their attacks were not pressed with vigour. The British casualties amounted to seven killed and 23 wounded.

A few days later a British reconnaissance advanced to Rifleman's Ridge but the approach proved abortive, the Ridge being too strongly held for investigation. An exchange of fire resulted in one man killed and three wounded. Boer casualties were one man killed and four wounded.

During the next three weeks the siege became increasingly monotonous and uneventful. The Boer burghers did nothing decisive against the garrison – only the guns remained active with the daily bombardment that caused little loss to the besieged. Towards the end of November another Long Tom appeared on Middle Hill, but after two days it was neutralised by two 6.3 inch [160 mm] howitzers termed "Castor" and "Pollux" and was moved to Telegraph Ridge. The big gun on Pepworth fired its last shot towards the end of November. It then appeared on an eminence, later called Gun Hill, closer to the town. Many of the Boers either moved to the Thukela River to oppose the relief force under General Sir Redvers Buller, VC, or went home, so that by early December there were 5 500 remaining around Ladysmith. This passive attitude did not escape the attention of the British.

The firing of the Long Tom and a 120 mm howitzer from Gun Hill had been so harassing that permission was sought to destroy them. For this purpose a force of 676 men drawn from the ranks of infantry, engineers and gunners moved out from Devonshire Post late in the evening of 7 December. The column advanced undetected, and after deploying some men at the foot of the hill, the rest climbed to the summit. A Boer sentry challenged the

assault force and a few shots were fired. The storming party broke into the emplacement of the Long Tom, and a little later a howitzer was found. Explosive charges were fixed to the breach and muzzles of both guns and successfully detonated. After shouting three cheers at the foot of the hill and collecting their wounded the British withdrew. The Long Tom, damaged in the raid, was removed to Pretoria for repair.

At daylight, encouraged by the success of the sortie the previous night, a mounted reconnaissance party left Ladysmith on the road to Newcastle. The Boers were alert, and with rifle and artillery fire compelled the party to withdraw with a loss of three men killed and 21 wounded.

On the night of 10 December another enterprise was undertaken by the British, this time against the Boer 120 mm howitzer on a hill to the north of the town, to be called Surprise Hill. Departing from King's Post, a 464-man force moved via Observation Hill and reached the foot of Surprise Hill in the early hours of 11 December. Once men had been positioned at the foot of the hill the remainder of the assault force climbed to the summit. The artillery piece was located but the explosive charges placed in the gun failed to ignite. A second fuse was set and it detonated. The men gave a cheer and turned for home. By now the Boers in the vicinity had become thoroughly alarmed. The assault party and their defensive detachment became hotly engaged with a Boer picket, later reinforced. The whole column fought its way out and marched back to Ladysmith. The British casualties were 20 killed or mortally wounded and 44 wounded and missing in action. The Boer loss was four killed and eight wounded or missing.

By mid-December both besiegers and the besieged turned to watch the events on the Thukela. Communication by means of heliograph

during the day and searchlights reflecting their beams from cloud at night from the direction of Colenso increased the tension of the garrison. Hopes were raised when distant artillery fire was heard towards the south. On 16 December White received a message from Buller that the attempt the day before to break through the Boer defences at Colenso, had failed. White was advised to destroy all his ammunition, burn his codes and was to make the best terms possible with the enemy. For White this was a bitter disillusionment; any surrender to the Boers was out of the question. Furthermore, he advised Buller to keep in touch with the Boers. In addition, White suggested a renewal of the attempt to relieve Ladysmith, while he undertook to maintain an active defence.

Deteriorating conditions

The news of Buller's defeat at Colenso brought an air of gloom and depression to the inhabitants of Ladysmith. The food supply was meagre. Bread and meat were rationed at reasonable prices for those people who could afford to pay. However, hundreds of the inhabitants had no money to pay for any rations and ran into debt. Those commodities not yet rationed reached alarming prices at the end of December 1899. Comforts were reduced for those besieged. Conditions began to deteriorate in other ways as well. There was a plague of flies. Colonel Park of the Devons wrote,

> "We have covered the mess shelter with strong disinfectants now to see if that will drive them away, as it is impossible to put a scrap of food into one's mouth without two or three going in too, and everything on the table is just a black buzzing mass of them."

Weighing and distributing rations during the siege.

There were hot times too when the temperature exceeded 40°C on three days. The tobacco supply became exhausted and the soldiers resorted to smoking dried sunflower leaves or tea leaves.

As a result of malnutrition and improper hygiene there was a rapid increase in the number of ill patients. Additional hospital tents at Intombi Spruit increased the bed capacity from 300 to 1 900 in less than three months. Although wounded soldiers continued to arrive in steady numbers, it was enteric fever and dysentery which reached epidemic proportions, eventually afflicting 1 700 soldiers and 1 800 civilians respectively. To feed such large numbers of patients, unable to take solid food, under conditions of a siege of uncertain duration, towards the end became a problem which could not be solved with satisfaction. By the end of the siege most luxuries had been consumed. The daily ration for fever patients was reduced to a minimum.

Lieutenant-General Sir George White's headquarters before it was shelled. The house still stands in Poort Road, albeit significantly altered.

The water supply, initially brought from the Klip River in the town, was sterilised and the mud removed by suspension. Later, cleaner water was obtained from five hogsheads dug in the Intombi Spruit yielding a daily supply of 67 000 litres. The hospital staff totalled 890 souls. In addition, for the sanitary work, 250 Indians and 131 Africans were employed, including a washing gang of 21. The rate at which patients died in the hospital demanded the services of 44 grave diggers for burials. All the dead were buried in a cemetery nearby.

At the end of December, White heard from Buller that the latter intended to begin another attempt at a relief via the upper Thukela at Potgieter's Drift. White promised to launch a supporting attack on the Boer perimeter, reiterating his confidence in his power to hold his own in Ladysmith. That ability was soon to be severely tested.

The first days of 1900 passed uneventfully. Only the usual shelling occupied the attention of the garrison resulting in two men killed and 11 wounded up to 5 January.

On New Year's day President SJP Kruger of the Zuid-Afrikaansche Republiek telegraphed Joubert emphasising the need to attack Ladysmith. Kruger pointed to the steady increase of British reinforcements that Buller was receiving. He maintained it was high time the siege was ended and the besieging commandos set free for service elsewhere. The Boer officers held a council-of-war on 3 January and agreed to launch an attack on Platrand (Wagon Hill and Caesar's Camp).

From the beginning of the siege the Boers considered Platrand, a ridge to the south of the town, as the key to Ladysmith. Its capture would make it possible to bring about the fall of the town.

In order to defend Wagon Point, Wagon Hill and Caesar's Camp, the Imperial troops manned picket lines along the southern crest-line and stone forts along the northern crest. All three prominences had gun pits or emplacements on them, several sheltering guns. By the evening of 5 January the Imperial troops totalled about 1 000 men and eight guns, all under the command of Colonel Ian Hamilton.

In the early hours of 6 January the Boers launched surprise attacks from the west and south-west on Wagon Hill and Wagon Point, and from the east and south-east on Caesar's Camp. At both extremities the Boers were able to drive the British out of their forward positions and secure footholds in parts of the defence lines. However, the

majority of Boers ordered to participate in the attacks failed to do so. The day saw some bitter fighting at very close quarters. The fighting came to an end as a typical rain and hailstorm broke over Ladysmith. This was accompanied by a dramatic charge by the Devons, driving the Boers out of a key position they had captured on Wagon Hill. As night fell the Boers retired to their siege lines. The British defence lines were intact, once again.

The cost to both the Boers and British had been high:

	Boers	British
Killed	62	168
Wounded	119	249
Total	181	417

For gallantry in the defence of the British lines on Platrand the Victoria Cross was awarded to: Lieutenant RJT Digby-Jones of the Royal Engineers and Trooper H Albrecht of the ILH, Lieutenant JEI Masterson of the Devonshire Regiment and Privates R Scott and J Pitts, both of the Manchester Regiment.

Siege rigours intensify

After 6 January the Boers abandoned the idea of taking Ladysmith by storm, and resolved to rely on bombardment and those potent allies of the besiegers – starvation, exhaustion and disease. By now the number of Boers necessary to preserve the cordon rarely exceeded 5 000 men, some authorities even placing the number as low as 3 500.

The remainder of January passed in relative stalemate. For the garrison there was the usual daily shelling and sharpshooting of the pickets. The British positions in Platrand received reinforcements. Elsewhere the perimeter of the town was further safeguarded by the

Slaughtering horses for food.

constant improvement of the defences. The casualties suffered by the garrison for the period 7 – 31 January were three killed and 21 wounded. However, the Ladysmith sicklist began to approach formidable proportions. By mid-January there were no fewer than 2 150 men in hospital, of whom 671 were cases of enteric fever.

In early January Buller began another attempt to reach Ladysmith. On the 12th, heliograph communication was established with the relief force at Potgieter's Drift on the upper Thukela. The days that followed were full of anxiety for the garrison. The Boers, apparently uneasy at the progress made by the British, kept up fire on the town for a whole day. Distant firing was heard which both encouraged and tormented the garrison. Full rations were restored and the troops were informed that relief was close at hand. Spioenkop, on 24 January, was seen to be

under smoke and exploding shells. The next day the British at Ladysmith looked expectantly for signs of an approaching relieving force. A large party of men were seen trekking northwards. But these were merely British soldiers captured at Spioenkop. Doubt began to assail the garrison, who were again reduced to half rations, and it became known later that Buller's force had suffered another reverse.

At the end of January, Macdonald recalls:

> "Everyone was back on half supplies and the disappointment was borne manfully. We got to the last stocks, the hard biscuit and tinned beef, which, with some coarse and mouldy mealie meal, stood between us and starvation.... The men were for the most part gaunt and gloomy, worn down by want of proper and sufficient provisions and the ceaseless manning of the rifle ridges."

The supply of drinking water in the town gave cause for concern. The garrison depended upon dirty water from the Klip River. By using Berkefeld filters, and later the use of an improvised system of filtration through wood ash, the soldiers were assured of a supply of 54 000 litres of clean water daily. The forage was so scarce that it became necessary to order the cavalry to turn loose their horses. The troopers, now dismounted, took post in the defences as infantry. From this time horses were sent to the commissariat to be slaughtered. In a locomotive shed, at the railway station, the horsemeat was converted into a paste called "chevril" which made a nourishing soup. Sausages and processed meats were also prepared; jellies and extracts were manufactured for use in the hospitals. To the officers of the Army Service Corps was given the responsibility of keeping the garrison and civilians alive. Thanks to their skill in utilising the meagre resources at their disposal, White

Civilians with precious supplies. Whisky was being offered for sale at £6 (R12) a bottle – the London price was 4 shillings.

was able to advance the date to which he calculated he would be able to hold out, from mid-January to 1 April.

Once more the garrison resigned itself to maintaining a passive defence. The physical strength of the infantrymen was dwindling daily, and the numbers of wounded or those who contracted diseases, rose sharply. At the Intombi Spruit hospitals the death rate reached eight per day. Macdonald again takes up the story:

> "With ever dwindling supplies, ever increasing hospitals, and with the graves at Intombi numbering over three hundred, not to mention the space that was being so rapidly filled in the town cemetery, it was not difficult to realise that in the latter days of January the besieged garrison of Ladysmith was racked by many doubts and anxieties."

The burial of the dead in the town's cemetery was done at night to avoid being targeted by the Boer gunners. Macdonald again:

> "There was little delay, for the graves were always ready, seven or eight at a time, and the white crosses grew thicker every day. The honours were sparse. No gun carriage, no coffin, no band playing the 'Dead March' and no last volley over the soldier's grave. There was a service, doubly impressive as read by the faint gleam of the dark lantern, and with the dimly-seen men in khaki gathered about the grave".

Meanwhile the Boers had not been idle. In mid-January, with the assistance of 1 200 black labourers, the Boers began to construct a wall of sandbags across the Klip River in a narrow defile near Mbulwana. It was hoped that the dammed water would flood the plain in which Ladysmith was situated and force the garrison to capitulate.

During the first week of February the relief force was engaged in operations at Vaalkrans and the Boers moved a Long Tom from Telegraph Ridge to the Thukela. The expectations of the garrison, looking for promising events to the south-west, were raised. When the troops failed to appear over the plain, depression set in again. Macdonald again:

> "The climax of stagnation was reached when men had no other aspiration but to lie down all day – no other desire than to be left to their own moody reflections. It was a dangerous stage – upon which fever and death quickly followed".

The bad news, or the dread of it, had a negative effect on the hospital patients. By 10 February the death rate had risen to 15 per day, bringing the total number of deaths at Intombi to 480. Rations were again reduced and the provision of more food was made possible by the daily slaughter of 70 horses.

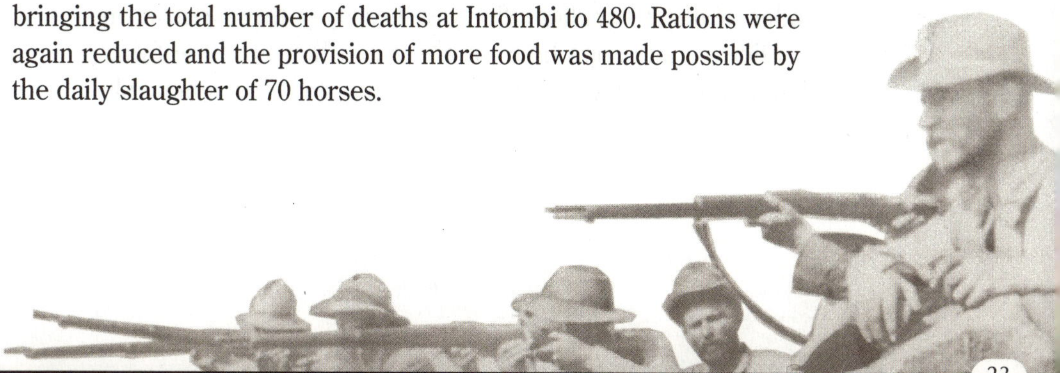

Medical personnel were kept increasingly busy as the siege wore on. Inadequate nutrition and unhygienic conditions took their toll, with the majority of patients suffering from enteric fever or dysentery rather than wounds.

On the 101st day of the siege, the Boers on Mbulwana called upon the signallers at Caesar's Camp and flashed the message, "101 not out", upon which came the reply, "Ladysmith still batting". By mid-February the last public auction was held, with food and tobacco being sold at high prices. The ordinary daily ration for a soldier now consisted of 450g of horsemeat, 225g biscuits, and small quantities of tea or coffee with sugar.

On 14 February the garrison received the welcome news of Lord Robert's army's entry into the Free State. Simultaneously the Boer gunners intensified their bombardment of the town. On the same day the thunder of distant artillery fire was heard by the garrison, in whom confidence and apprehension alternated hourly as the firing seemed now to be drawing closer, now receding, and most ominously

of all, to subside altogether. Boer commandos were seen to come and go. On the 17th shells were observed bursting to the south along Cingolo and Monte Cristo. The bombardment of the town, which never ceased, increased in severity. The British responded from Caesar's Camp on the crowd of men seen working at the dam site and thereby drawing upon themselves the fire of Long Tom on Mbulwana. In an effort to avoid the British bombardment, construction of the dam was switched to night time. However, these activities did not escape the attention of the British gunners. Problems of labour shortage hampered the construction, with the result that daylight work was resumed. At the end of February, with a reduced labour force, the Boers estimated the wall was scheduled for completion in early March.

On 23 and 24 February the sound of battle continued to the south. On the 25th the sound of firing died away, and the garrison ignorant of its cause – which was the observance of an armistice – regarded the silence with foreboding as an indication of yet another failure. The reduction of rations to a quarter of the normal scale seemed to confirm that disaster had befallen the relief force. On the 26th distant firing arose again, and swelled to an incessant and tremendous roar on the next day, and subsided into silence once more by nightfall. Early on the 28th the roads to the north were shrouded in dust through which Boers were seen heading northward. On Mbulwana Boer gunners, having fired one last shell from their Long Tom, were seen dismantling the weapon, and though the British artillery fired at its emplacement, the Boers managed to remove it.

In the late afternoon a group of horsemen were seen galloping near Intombi camp. Relief was at hand. Initially this small force was seen by only a few. Sometime later they crossed the Klip River and made their way through a throng of cheering soldiers. The siege, which had lasted 118 days, was over. The casualties for the garrison for February were one man killed and 18 wounded.

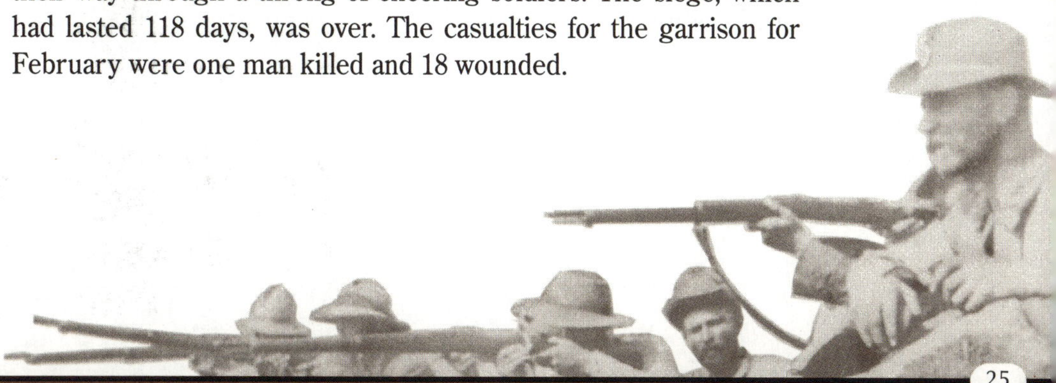

Africans were used to carry messages through the siege lines. This messenger is about to take a message into Ladysmith, concealed in his garments.

Next morning (1 March 1900) Buller paid a short visit to Ladysmith. A large convoy of wagons, loaded with food and medical supplies, was driven in during the day and the goods distributed. During the morning a flying column was ordered to intercept the retreating Boers. This force, being weak both in numbers and physical condition, moved as far as Pepworth Hill and became slightly engaged, but then withdrew into the town.

On 2 March Buller established his headquarters in the town, and the next day led the relieving force through the streets. The British force then dispersed into various bivouacs near the town, which were cleaner and healthier.

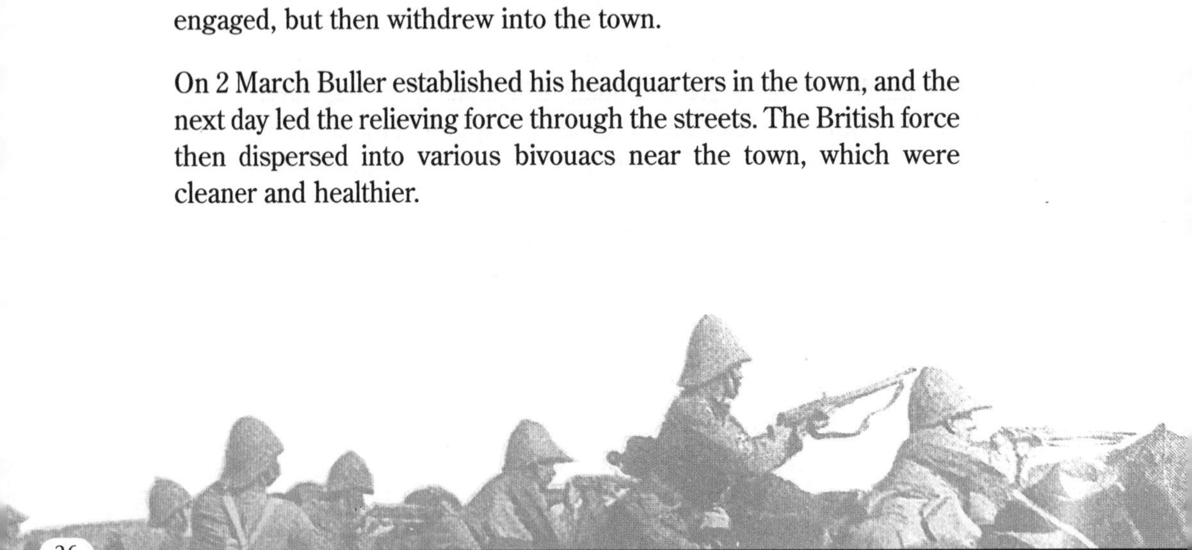

On 3 March Buller's relieving army made its formal entry into Ladysmith passing between White's men who lined the streets. It was a stirring moment full of the pomp and circumstance of war; full also of its pathos, as men recognised old friends and comrades in arms, or looked vainly down the ranks for those whom they expected, but whom they were destined not to see again.

At the beginning of March there were almost 2 800 ill and wounded soldiers, and the evacuation of these patients presented a major problem. Because of the destruction of the bridges and culverts to the south, the transport of patients was hampered until the railway line was made clear. These problems were finally overcome, and in the last week of March the Intombi hospitals were emptied of patients.

During the siege it was estimated that 18 000 – 20 000 shells were fired into the town. For the same period the British artillery replied with 6 096 projectiles. The number of deaths to the besieged was 833 soldiers, including civilians in military employ; 270 were killed in action or died of wounds (218 of these in assaults and sorties, 62 from casual bombardment) while 563 died from diseases. In addition ten men were missing in action. There were 11 135 admissions alone to Intombi hospitals. The total number of deaths to the civilian population was 54.

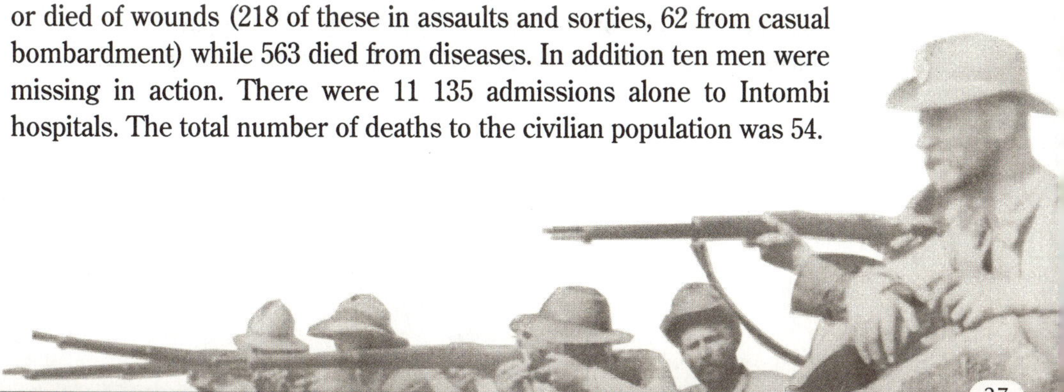

Military hospital on the Oval in the centre of Ladysmith. A shopping complex has been built over this open ground.

Ladysmith today

Ladysmith, like many other South African towns, has seen much change in the intervening 100 years. A few buildings which stood in 1899-1900 are still to be seen. These include the Royal Hotel, both residences occupied by Sir George White, the Town Hall, the All Saint's Church and the Convent (now the La Verna hospital).

The Royal Hotel, thought to have been a target of the Boer gunners, has been enlarged, notably with a longer facade bordering on Murchison Street. In front of the hotel, embedded in the pavement, is the base of a shell which killed Dr AC Stark on 18 November 1899.

The first house occupied by the British commander, although it has undergone modification, is to be seen at 16 Poort Road. After the building was hit by a shell the British commander moved to safer quarters in Tatham Street on Convent Hill.

Although the frontage of the Town Hall is the same as it was in 1899, the interior has undergone extensive modification. What used to be a hospital ward is now a courtyard bounded by corridors, whilst to the rear of the building, stands a large hall.

All Saint's Church in Murchison Street was damaged by a Boer shell on 20 November 1899. It penetrated the roof of the porch and destroyed a wall. The hole in the roof was repaired and the patchwork is still visible, while the remains of the shell are mounted in the rebuilt wall. Inside the church are memorial panels of Italian marble mounted in the transepts. Engraved in the panels are the names of 2 640 soldiers who died in the siege and the relief of Ladysmith. There are also the names of 54 civilians who died in the siege. In addition there is a panel containing 154 names of the men who lost their lives during the whole war whilst serving in the 19th Hussars. All the engraving, done superbly, was performed on location by Walter Chatham (1878-1958). In the garden of the church is an obelisk to the memory of the men of the 18th Hussars who died in the war.

Apart from the town cemetery in the town (in which military burials were also performed), the creation of military cemeteries has resulted from the proximity of military hospitals or the dead collected at battle sites. On Tchrengula there are two mass graves: one containing 40 bodies of the 1st Gloucester Regiment, and another containing ten men of the 1st Irish Fusiliers and two artillerymen of the 10th Mountain Battery RGA. All these men died in the Boer attack on the British position on Tchrengula (30 October 1899).

Nurse Kate Driver nursed the sick and wounded throughout the siege, mainly at Intombi Camp. She experienced at first hand the effects of war and in her memoirs wrote, "The blind brutality of war is alien to the spirit of most people in the world."

At the foot of Surprise Hill there were originally the scattered graves of the men of the 2nd Rifle Brigade who fell in action whilst returning from the sortie on the night of 11-12 December 1899. Today only a stone cairn, on which appear the nine names of those killed, marks the locality near where the action took place. The soldiers' remains were exhumed and reinterred in Tin Town cemetery. Lieutenant GCD Fergusson, the only officer mortally wounded, was carried into Ladysmith and buried in the town cemetery the same evening.

After the siege was raised, those soldiers who contracted illness or were wounded were moved to more healthy surroundings. A military hospital was established near Observation Hill, and those patients who died in it were buried in two cemeteries on the Niblick Koppies. Tin Town cemetery contains the bodies of 103 soldiers, some of whom were originally buried here, and the remainder exhumed from Niblick Koppies and the scattered graves of the Rifle Brigade near Surprise Hill.

The town cemetery contains military burials which took place during the entire war, although most date to the period of the siege. A large monument commemorates the 473 soldiers who lie buried in two military precincts. All the metal crosses have been removed while the marble or granite gravestones have been moved to the perimeter.

The military cemetery at Intombi Spruit was started in early November 1899 and continued to receive burials for three weeks after the siege was raised. Today 659, including 15 civilians, lie buried at Intombi. Over the years, other ideas have evolved for the maintenance of the graves. All the metal markers have been removed, and a single monument on which are inscribed the names of all those who are interred, has been erected. The marble and granite headstones have been moved from their original positions and placed astride the monument.

Around the former British perimeter stand several monuments. On Tunnel Hill a stone obelisk commemorates the 1st Liverpool Regiment who held this post for a while. On it are inscribed 174 names of the men of the regiment who died in the Anglo-Boer War. Near the top of Junction Hill, a shield of a 4.7-inch naval gun, commemorates the site of the "Lady Anne" battery. The gun emplacement took a direct hit of a Long Tom shell fired from Pepworth Hill mortally wounding Lieutenant FG Egerton. The suburb Egerton and Egerton Primary School now perpetuate his

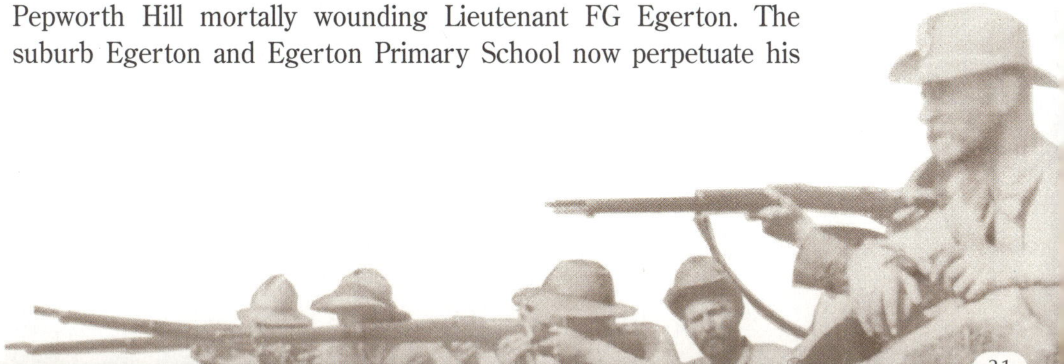

The Boers dammed the Klip River near Intombi camp in an attempt to flood Ladysmith. This project ran out of time. A large team of Africans assisted with the building of this dam.

name. On Gordon Hill a stone obelisk stands to the memory of the cavalrymen of the 5th Dragoon Guards. On Observation Hill is a memorial to the men of the 1st Leicestershire Regiment.

Between Red Hill and Signpost Ridge is a marble monument to the memory of 18 men of the 1st Royal Irish Fusiliers who died in Ladysmith. Nearby stands a stone cairn, which marks the spot where Lieutenant Colonel WH Dick-Cunyngham VC, 2nd Gordon Highlanders, was mortally wounded. He fell after being hit by a bullet fired at a range of 2 700 metres during the Boer attack on Platrand (6 January 1900).

At the eastern extremity of Maiden Castle at Fly Kraal stands a stone cairn to the memory of some Gordon Highlanders who camped here during the siege.

The scene of the big Boer attack and the successful British defence on Platrand (6 January 1900) is characterised by several monuments and graves. Along the road to the summit of the heights a cemetery can be seen at the foot of Wagon Hill. It contains the graves of 78 Imperial soldiers including Tpr Albrecht VC whose remains, as well as those of his fellow Imperial Light Horse, were reinterred from the summit of Wagon Hill. On Caesar's Camp there is the large Burgher memorial to the memory of the 781 Boers who lost their lives in Natal during the war. The mortal remains of 313 men, exhumed from the Natal battlefields, have been placed in a crypt around which are several pillars containing panels of the men's names who died in a particular battle. The gravestones, brought in from various sites, have been embedded in a wall. Manchester Fort, built by two companies of the 1st Manchester Regiment, was occupied up to the time of the battle of Platrand, thereafter by the 18th Hussars until the end of the siege. Near the eastern extremity of Caesar's Camp stands a stone obelisk to the men of the 1st Manchester Regiment. On it are 113 names of men of the regiment who fell in action or died of disease in and near Ladysmith. Mention is also made of the 172 men who were killed in action or died of disease during the entire war. In the vicinity are several graves and monuments: a mass grave contains 13 bodies of soldiers of the Manchester Regiment and one of the 2nd Rifle Brigade, while nearby another mass grave contains 18 men of the Rifle Brigade whose names have been recorded on a cairn next to the cemetery. On Wagon Hill stand several monuments each marking the scene of a particular event. The soldiers of the 1st Devonshire Regiment who fell in the gallant and successful charge (which dislodged the Boers from the southern crest) are remembered by a large stone obelisk near the scene of the action. Nearby stands a tall marble obelisk marking the spot of the Imperial Light Horse redoubt where the ILH withstood the brunt of the Boer attacks. The bodies of the ILH were originally buried at the spot, but were exhumed and reinterred in the Wagon Hill cemetery. In the vicinity stands a

marble cross marking the spot where the Earl of Ava fell mortally wounded while carrying a message to the ILH lines. Between Wagon Hill and Wagon Point is a granite slab to the memory of the Reverend JD Kestell describing the compassion shown by him to the wounded, both Briton and Boer. On Wagon Point stands a stone cairn to the memory of Assistant Field Cornet JH de Villiers who fell after he led an attack by a small band of Free Staters on the 4.7-inch naval gun emplacement. The emplacement is in a good state of repair and stands near a cairn to the memory of some Royal Engineers (including Lieutenant RJT Digby Jones VC) who fell in this vicinity. At the western extremity of the height is a stone cairn to Sergeant Webb of the 18th Hussars who fell in action at this point. He is buried in the town cemetery.

A small cemetery in Riebeeck Park contains a soldier of the 5th Lancers who died of wounds received at Wagon Hill.

On Middle Hill is a cairn marking the spot near where Major Taunton lost his life, together with several other soldiers, in their foray into "Long Valley" on 3 November 1899.

Forces engaged

Imperial

	Effective in Siege			
Cavalry	**Beginning**	**End**	**Deaths**	**Guns**
Commanding: Maj-Gen Brocklehurst				
5th Dragoon Guards	515	372	31	1
5th Lancers	489	360	27	1

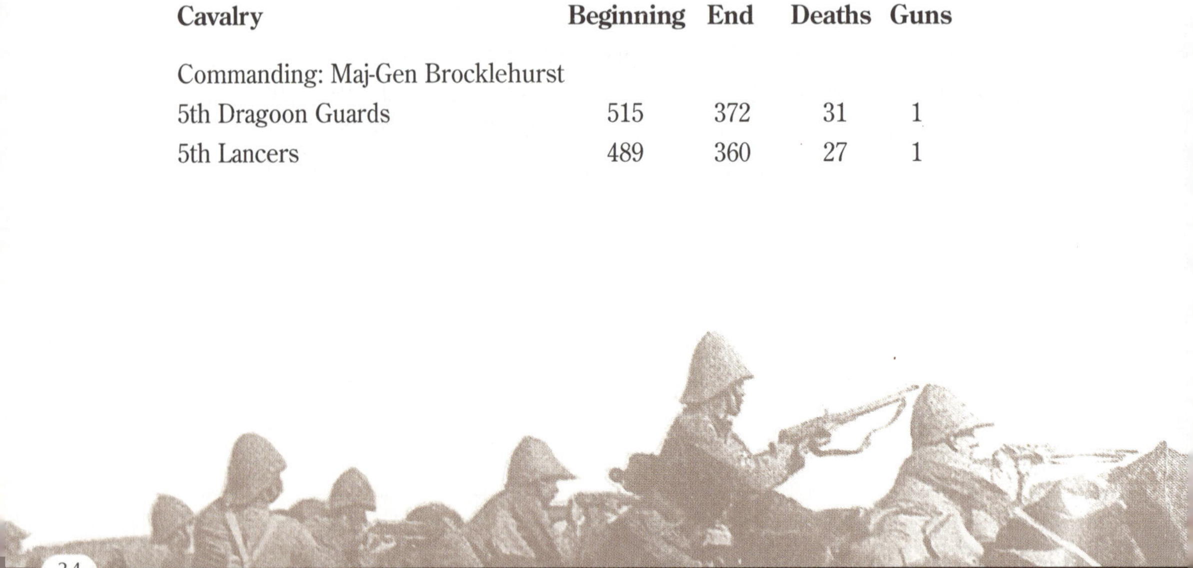

	Beginning	End	Deaths	Guns
18th Hussars	435	229	17	0
19th Hussars	560	195	50	1
Imperial Light Horse	436	126	44	0

Guns: Machine.

Royal Artillery

Commanding: Col CMH Downing

	Beginning	End	Deaths	Guns
13th Batt Royal Field Artillery	177	155	5	6
21st Batt Royal Field Artillery	167	126	8	6
42nd Batt Royal Field Artillery	167	121	6	6
53rd Batt Royal Field Artillery	165	120	4	6
67th Batt Royal Field Artillery	169	138	4	6
69th Batt Royal Field Artillery	168	140	7	6
1st Brigade Ammunition Column	106	84	3	-
2nd Brigade Ammunition Column	96	79	3	-
10th Mtn Batt Royal Garrison Artillery	86	73	4	2
Maxim Nordenfeldt detachment	24	23	0	2
Howitzer detachment	19	20	0	2
In store				4

Guns. RFA: 15-pdr Armstrong

RGA: 2.5-in

Maxim-Nordenfeldt: 37mm

Howitzer: 6.3-in

	Beginning	End	Deaths	Guns
Royal Engineers, 23 Co	195	143	23	-
Royal Engineers, Telegraph Bn	57	46	3	-
Royal Engineers, Balloon Sect	32	23	2	-

Infantry	Beginning	End	Deaths	Guns
Commanding Lieutenant Col AER Curran				
7th Infantry Brigade				
Commanding: Col ISM Hamilton				
1st Bn Manchester	864	645	65	1
1st Bn R Irish Fusiliers (2 Cos)	238	189	26	1
2nd Bn Rifle Brigade (7 Cos)	778	551	75	0
2nd Bn Gordon Highlanders	828	744	26	1
Guns: Machine				
8th Infantry Brigade				
Commanding: Maj-Gen F Howard.				
1st Bn Liverpool	906	676	39	1
1st Bn Leicestershire	981	778	46	0
2nd Bn King's Royal Rifle Corps	774	516	68	0
Guns: Machine.				
Divisional Troops				
Commanding: Col WG Knox				
1st Bn Devonshire	851	731	48	1
1st Bn Gloucestershire (4 Cos)	452	376	32	0
1st Bn King's Royal Rifle Corps	685	506	48	1
2nd Bn R Dublin Fusiliers ($^1/_2$ Co)	58	44	1	0
Guns: Machine				
Army Service Corps, no 4 Co	101	85	5	-
Commanding: Col EWD Ward				
Royal Army Medical Corps	208	178	4	-
including field hospitals				
Commanding: LT Col R Exham				

	Beginning	End	Deaths	Guns
Army Ordnance Corps and	51	41	2	-
Indian Ordnance Dept	19	18	0	-
Commanding: Maj WC Saville				
Royal Navy	280	216	27	10
Commanding: The Hon H Lambton				
Guns: Two 4.7-in Naval				
Four Naval 12-pdr				
Four machine				
Volunteers				
Commanding: Col W Royston				
Staff	71	34	0	0
Natal Carbineers	348	164	16	2
Natal Mounted Rifles	173	112	5	0
Border Mounted Rifles	248	121	17	2
Natal Police	73	34	4	0
Natal Naval Volunteers	67	55	6	3
Ladysmith Town Guard	120	119	1	4
Guns: Natal Naval Vols:				
Other units: Machine				
Staff and miscellaneous	270	250	4	-
Commanding: Lieutenant-Gen Sir GS White VC				

		Beginning	End	Deaths	Guns
TOTAL:		13 496	10 164	833	73
Killed in action	211				
Died of wounds	59				
Died of disease	563*				
Missing in action	10				

* = includes 22 followers.

Boer

Note. *All details refer to early November 1899. The number of men, quantity and placement of artillery varied throughout the siege.*

Thornhill's Kop, Bell's Kop, Surprise Hill, Pepworth Hill:

Pretoria Commando 1 492 men.

Pepworth Hill:

Transvaal Police ? men, Transvaal Staatsartillerie 320 under SPE Trichardt; Irish Brigade 300; Ermelo Commando 580.

Long Hill to Lombard's Kop:

Lydenburg Commando 1 100.

Artillery: Three 120 mm howitzers, four hand maxims.

Lombard's Kop, Gun Hill, Umbrella Hill:

Heidelberg Commando 1 700.

Artillery: Two Krupp guns

Mbulwana southwards to Fourie Spruit under General Lucas Meyer:

Commandos of Wakkerstroom 800, Vryheid 944, Utrecht 900, Krugersdorp 800, Middelburg ?, German Corps from Pretoria ?.

Artillery: Four Krupp guns, two 75 mm Creusot guns, One Pom Pom, one maxim.

Telegraph Ridge and westward to the Klip River:

Commandos of Kroonstad 2 500, Bethlehem ?,

Rifleman's Ridge:

Vrede Commando ?.

Lancer's Hill:

Heilbron Commando 1 670

Middle Hill:

Harrismith Commando 915

Artillery: One Long Tom (see below).

End Hill, (east of) Middle Hill to Fourie's Spruit:

Winburg Commando 2 114.

Note. *A Long Tom appeared on 8 November 1899 on Mbulwana and remained there until the end of the siege. A second Long Tom appeared on Middle Hill on 27 November 1899, but was neutralised by British artillery and removed after two days. A third Long Tom appeared on Pepworth Hill on 29 October 1899, reappeared on Gun Hill on 24 November 1899. Damaged in a raid on 7-8 December 1899 it was removed to Pretoria, repaired, and sent to Kimberley.*

Additional Reading

Breytenbach, J.H. *Die Geskiedenis van die Tweede Vryheidsoorlog in Suid Afrika* Vol II & III (Pretoria, Die Staatsdrukker, 1969-1978).

Gibson, G.F. *The Story of the Imperial Light Horse* (London, J & D, 1937).

Griffith, K. *Thank God we kept the flag flying* (London, Hutchinson, 1974).

MacDonald, D. *How we kept the flag flying* (London, Ward, Locke, 1900).

Maurice, F. and Grant, M.H. *History of the War in South Africa* (London, Hurst and Blackett, 1907) Vol. II.

Nevison, H.W. *Ladysmith: The Diary of a Siege* (London, Methuen, 1900).

Pakenham, Thomas. *The Boer War* (Johannesburg, Jonathan Ball, 1979).

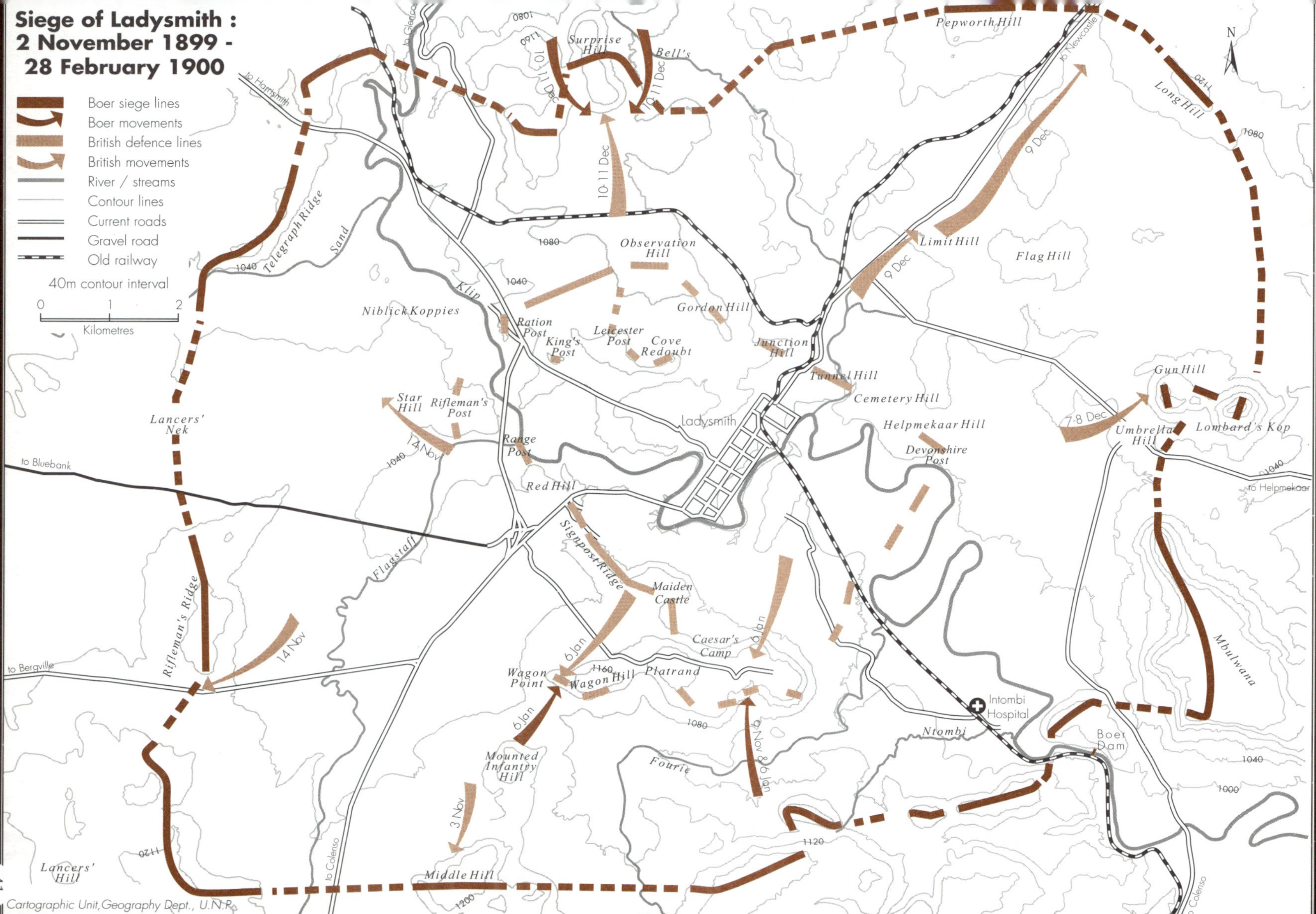

Cartographic Unit, Geography Dept., U.N.P.

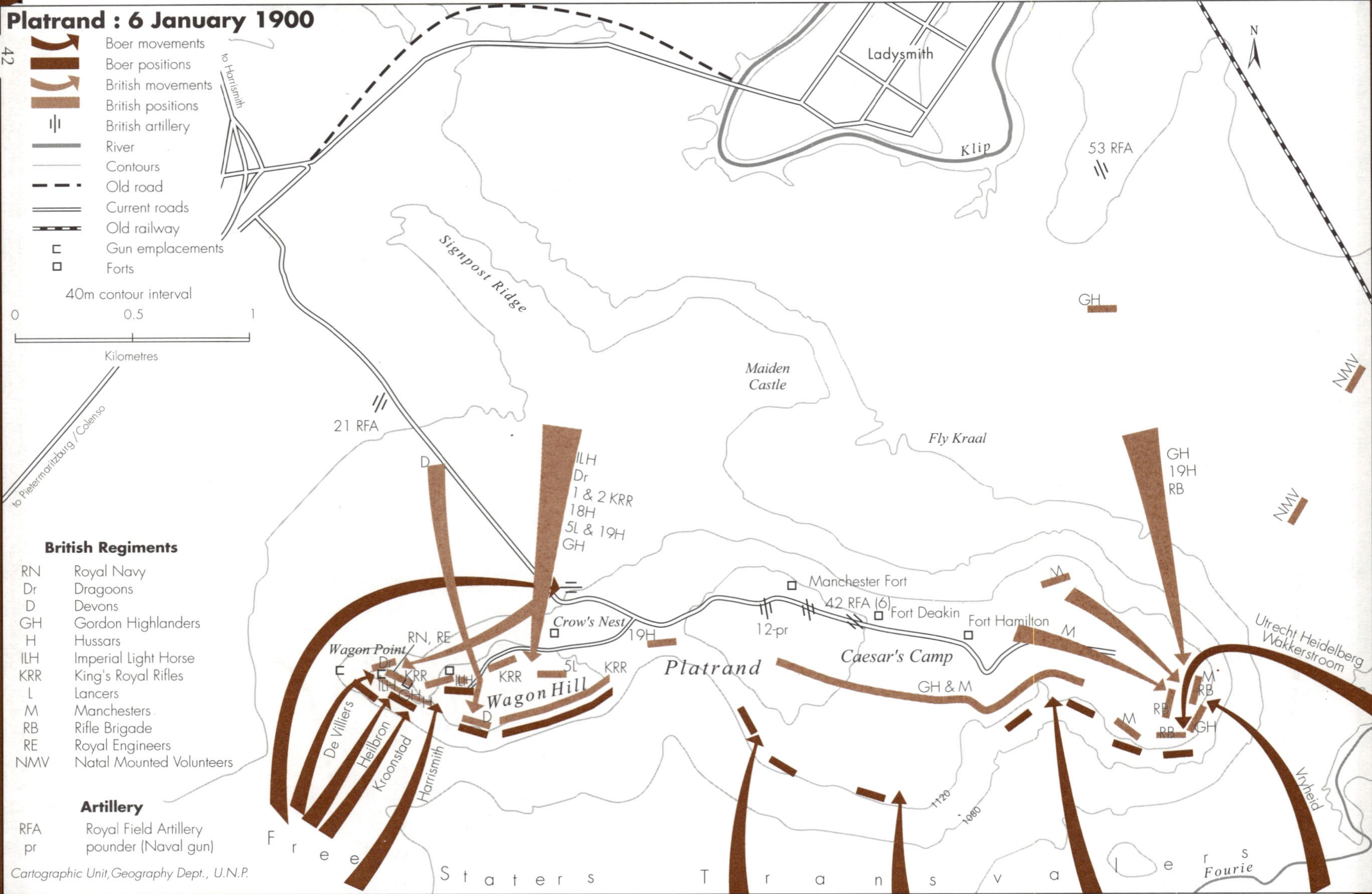
Platrand : 6 January 1900
Boer movements
Boer positions
British movements
British positions
British artillery
River
Contours
Old road
Current roads
Old railway
Gun emplacements
Forts
40m contour interval
0
0.5
1
Kilometres
to Harrismith
to Pietermaritzburg / Colenso
British Regiments
RN Royal Navy
Dr Dragoons
D Devons
GH Gordon Highlanders
H Hussars
ILH Imperial Light Horse
KRR King's Royal Rifles
L Lancers
M Manchesters
RB Rifle Brigade
RE Royal Engineers
NMV Natal Mounted Volunteers
Artillery
RFA Royal Field Artillery
pr pounder (Naval gun)
Cartographic Unit, Geography Dept., U.N.P.
Ladysmith
Klip
53 RFA
Signpost Ridge
Maiden Castle
Fly Kraal
21 RFA
ILH
Dr
1 & 2 KRR
18H
5L & 19H
GH
GH
19H
RB
NMV
NMV
Manchester Fort
42 RFA (6)
Fort Deakin
Fort Hamilton
Crow's Nest
12-pr
Caesar's Camp
Platrand
Wagon Point
Wagon Hill
RN, RE
KRR
ILH
5L
19H
GH & M
De Villiers
Heilbron
Kroonstad
Harrismith
Utrecht Heidelberg
Wakkerstroom
Vryheid
Fourie
1120
1080
Free Staters
Transvaalers

Ladysmith and Surrounds: Memorials, Graves

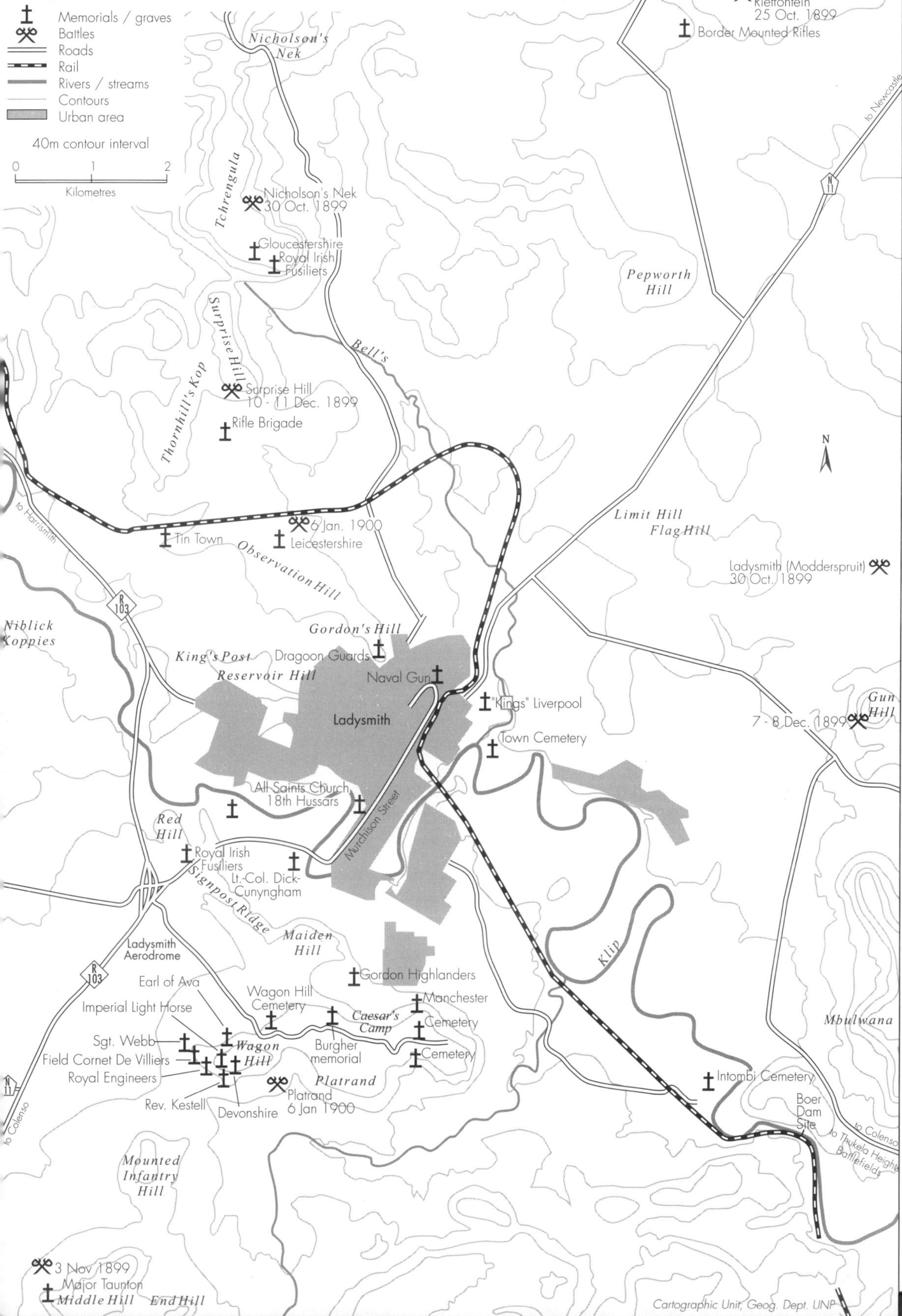